THE**COMPLETE**GUIDE**TO** **PLAYING**BLUES**GUITAR**

Book Three: Melodic Phrasing

JOSEPH**ALEXANDER**

FUNDAMENTAL**CHANGES**

The Complete Guide to Playing Blues Guitar

Book Three - Beyond Pentatonics

Published by www.fundamental-changes.com

ISBN: 978-1-78933-037-3

www.fundamental-changes.com

Twitter: **@guitar_joseph**

Over 10,000 fans on Facebook: FundamentalChangesInGuitar

Instagram: **FundamentalChanges**

For over 250 Free Guitar Lessons with Videos Check Out

www.fundamental-changes.com

Contents

Introduction

I originally intended for this series to be just two books, the first focusing on blues guitar rhythm and the second focusing on soloing. I'm extremely proud of both books, however there were some things that I didn't have room to cover in enough detail:

1) Different scales and approaches you can use for soloing

2) How to articulate or target chord changes in your solos to give depth, interest and emotion to your melodies.

Scale Choice

The soloing concepts in Book Two were all about rhythm and phrasing. First and foremost, I believe that rhythm and feel are much more important in authentic blues soloing than scale choice. This is because even if we know every possible scale that could be used, they won't sound good if played with poor rhythm, phrasing and feel.

However, once we can play solos with great feel, then a detailed knowledge of scale choice options and their unique colours is essential if we are to be truly expressive.

There are many different scales that can be used over a 12-bar blues. Some can be used over the whole progression and some sound better when played over just one or two chords.

We will study the most common scales in turn and learn their theory and application, with many useful licks given for each one. The main thing to discover is the sound of the scales. Each one brings different colours and inflection to our music, and subtly alters the mood of our solos.

We end up with a wide variety of soloing possibilities, so to help internalise and organise this information I have included a set of soloing schemes suggesting useful scale applications and licks for each section of the blues progression.

Chord Articulation (Note Targeting)

Have you ever wondered how the great blues guitar players always seem to hit exactly the right note at exactly the right time? You know, that one note in a solo that made you go "Ahhhh!"?

The secret to this seemingly magical technique is to *target* specific notes exactly when the chords change.

The targeted note is often (but not always) an important arpeggio tone in the new chord, and by playing it at a specific time it outlines part of the underlying chord progression of the solo.

If overdone, our lines can start to sound a bit jazzy, but used with subtlety and discretion we can play emotive and articulate solos over any chord progression.

Often, amateur blues guitarists drape the whole blues chord progression with the tonic Minor Pentatonic scale, but in this book you will learn that by changing just one or two notes in our solos we can give a profound new level of depth to our music.

When the concept of target note articulation is combined with interesting scale choices, we start to play more meaningful, emotional and melodically interesting solos. Then, combine these approaches with all the rhythm and phrasing techniques from Book Two and you'll be well on your way to mastering blues guitar soloing.

Chord articulation is the most immediate and effective way to bring new life and soul into a solo. By becoming aware of just a few melodic possibilities that are presented as the chords change, we can make a profound and emotive melodic difference to our solos. It doesn't take much work to alter just one or two notes in your solo to highlight the harmony and create your own little moments of magic.

The ideas contained here are the icing on the cake. They should be used with subtlety and at specific times to draw the listener's attention to certain notes and to create different feelings. When overused they can make a solo sound contrived and pre-planned.

It is likely that over 80% your blues soloing will still be Minor Pentatonic/Blues scale-based because, these scales form the traditional vocabulary of the blues. However, with restrained use of the melodic techniques here, you will quickly progress far beyond your current ability.

Remember, rhythm, phrasing and feel always comes first. If you haven't checked out Book Two in this series yet I highly recommend doing so, as it focuses exclusively on those skills.

Have fun and good luck!

Joseph

Get the Audio

The audio files for this book are available to download for free from **www.fundamental-changes.com** and the link is in the top right corner. Simply select this book title from the drop-down menu and follow the instructions to get the audio.

We recommend that you download the files directly to your computer, not to your tablet, and extract them there before adding them to your media library. You can then put them on your tablet, iPod or burn them to CD. On the download page there is a help PDF and we also provide technical support via the contact form.

Kindle / eReaders

To get the most out of this book, remember that you can double tap any image to enlarge it. Turn off 'column viewing' and hold your kindle in landscape mode.

Be Social

Twitter: **@guitar_joseph**

FB: **FundamentalChangesInGuitar**

Instagram: **FundamentalChanges**

For over 250 Free Guitar Lessons with Videos Check out

www.fundamental-changes.com

Part One - Chord Articulation: Playing the Changes

Chapter One: Outlining the Chord I to Chord IV Movement

Many people solo over the 12-bar blues progression exclusively with the Minor Pentatonic scale. In this book, we will pay much more attention to the notes contained in each individual chord of the progression and adjust our soloing approach slightly for each one. By targeting specific notes in each chord, we break free from Minor Pentatonic playing and bring emotion, articulation and some great-sounding note choices to our solos.

We will begin by examining the first significant chord change in the blues progression. This chord change is from chord I (A7) to chord IV (D7) and occurs in bar five.

Although there is sometimes a change from A7 to D7 in the first two bars of the blues, the point where the listener first really *feels* the change to the IV chord (D7) is in bar five.

Let's look at the actual notes contained in the chords of A7 and D7, and more specifically how these notes move when the chords change. By targeting the notes that change between the two chords, we can find new, effective melody notes to use in our solos.

This concept can be seen in the following diagram:

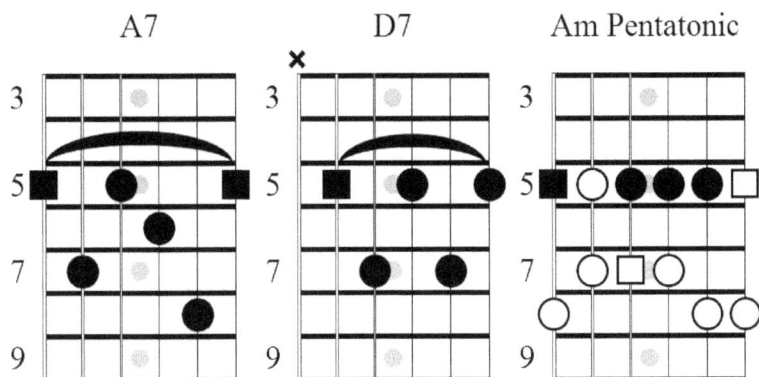

Compare the notes in the A7 diagram to the ones in D7. Pay particular attention to the following:

1) In the A7 chord, the note played on the 3rd string, 6th fret (C#) *descends* by a semitone to become C on the 5th fret in the D7 chord.

2) In the A7 chord, the note on the 2nd string, 8th fret (G) descends by a semitone to the 7th fret in the D7 chord (F#).

3) In the Minor Pentatonic diagram, notice that the it does not contain the F# note mentioned in point 2.

The notes that change between A7 and D7 are called *guide tones*, and they are the secret to melodically outlining this chord change in a solo.

I like to keep theory to a minimum, but for a broader understanding of this subject it is important to know that guide tones are the 3rd and 7th intervals of any chord. The 3rd and 7th are the notes that define the chord name and character. They are even more important than the root note when it comes to describing the chord.

To outline, or *describe* a chord in a solo we can always play some of its arpeggio notes (an arpeggio is simply the notes of a chord played one at a time), but the most powerful and descriptive notes to target are always the 3rd and 7th.

The strongest notes to target in A7 are the C# and the G (3 and b7).

Interval	Root	3	5	b7
Note	A	C#	E	G

The strongest notes to target in D7 are F# and C

Interval	Root	3	5	b7
Note	D	F#	A	C

What we're most interested in is how the individual notes move when the chord changes from A7 to D7.

When playing a blues solo, until now you have probably only used the A Minor Pentatonic scale to solo over the D7 chord. There is nothing wrong with that, but let's take a deeper look and compare the notes of the D7 chord to the notes of the A Minor Pentatonic scale:

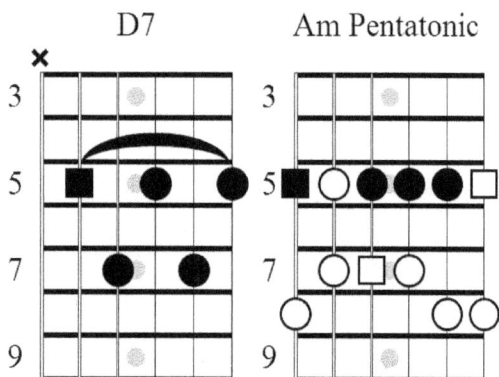

Look at the notes on the 2nd (B) string. You can see that the D7 chord contains the important F# note on the 7th fret and that it is not contained in the Minor Pentatonic scale. Instead, the Minor Pentatonic contains a note on the 2nd string, 8th fret instead (G). Remember that the note G is the b7 guide tone of A7.

The F# (3rd of the D7 chord) is an important guide tone in the chord of D7 (it is the 3rd) and helps define the D7 sound.

To outline the chord of D7 in our solo, simply target the F# guide tone as the A7 chord changes to D7.

The b7 note G in the A7 chord falls by a semitone to target the F# as the chord changes to D7. By targeting that changing note in the solo melody, we outline the chord change.

Listen first, and then play the following line along with backing track one. Notice how the final note in bar three descends by a semitone to land on (target) the F# and how this note choice highlights and strengthens the D7 sound.

Example 1a:

This kind of melodic movement is so strong that you can force your listener to hear the chord change when there is no band or backing track playing. Try playing the previous lick unaccompanied and see if your ears hear the chord change.

Targeting guide tones is a powerful tool and by learning how to use this technique on any chord change we can play emotive, articulate solos.

The reason this sounds so strong is because until this point we have not heard the note F# in the melody.

As long as we hit the 3rd of D7 just as the chord changes, we can target it in any way we like. Let's target the 3rd of the D7 chord with a slide from below.

Example 1b:

Here are a few more lines to help you target the 3rd of the D7 (F#) on the 2nd string:

Example 1c:

In example 1d I delay hitting the F# until later in the bar. This is bit more subtle than playing the guide tone on the first beat of the bar.

Example 1d:

The 3rd of D7 can also be targeted in the lower octave. This is a little harder to see but if we examine the arpeggios of A7 and D7 it becomes clearer.

An arpeggio is simply the notes of a chord played in sequence. Here are the arpeggios for A7 and D7:

A7 Arpeggio   D7 Arpeggio

In the A7 chord look at the note G on the 4th string, 5th fret. Notice how it falls to the F# 4th string, 4th fret in the D7 chord. This is the same movement we played before, just in a lower octave.

Here is a simple idea to highlight this change in the lower octave:

Example 1e:

As with example 1a, example 1e targets the major 3rd of D7 on beat one. See how many ways you can find to target the 3rd as the chord changes to D7.

Ending the melody as soon as you hit a target note sounds a bit obvious and forced.

The following ideas build some melodic momentum throughout the chord change. You will see that once you have targeted the 3rd of D7 it is easy to continue with an A Minor Pentatonic idea over the D7 chord.

Example 1f:

Example 1g:

In example 1h I bend the minor 3rd of D7 (F) up a semitone towards the F#.

You could view this idea as playing *D Minor Pentatonic* over the D7 chord and adding a bluesy bend just as you would with the A Minor Pentatonic scale over the A7 chord.

Example 1h:

Targeting the major 3rd as the chord changes to D7 is a strong melodic idea because it keeps the melody of our solo aligned closely to the harmonic backing (chord). It can be overused so use it sparingly.

The major 3rd is not the only chord tone that moves by a semitone between A7 and D7.

Look at the 3rd string, 6th fret (C#) on the A7 chord.

Can you see how the dark dot falls by a semitone to the 3rd string 5th fret (C) on the D7 chord?

The C# is the major 3rd of the A7 chord and it falls by a semitone to a C natural in the D7 chord.

Even though the C# note does not occur in the A Minor Pentatonic scale you will probably already hint at it over A7 chord, possibly without knowing it.

Here is a short section from **Complete Guide to Blues Guitar Book Two: Melodic Phrasing** where I talk extensively about bending the minor 3rd (C) of the Minor Pentatonic scale slightly towards the major 3rd (C#) of the A7 chord:

"The chords in a blues are normally played as Dominant 7. These are a special kind of major-type chord and contain a major 3rd. The Minor Pentatonic scale, however, contains a minor 3rd (b3) interval. This can be seen clearly on the guitar when you view a dominant 7 chord next to the Minor Pentatonic scale.

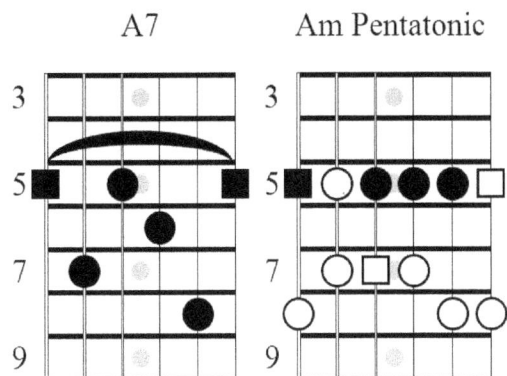

A7   Am Pentatonic

Notice that the C# on the 3rd (6th fret on the 3rd string) of the A7 chord isn't included in the A Minor Pentatonic scale. Instead, it has a C on the 3rd string 5th fret. These two notes, a semitone apart (C# in the chord and C in the melody) will clash and most musicians would say this is undesirable. It certainly isn't the greatest sound if you just 'sit' on the minor 3rd and don't manipulate it in any way.

As you can hear that this isn't the greatest sound in the world!

Example 1i:

Guitarists get around this problem by giving the minor 3rd (C) a little bend up towards the major 3rd (C#).

To do this, use your 1st finger to bend the string towards the floor to slightly raise its pitch towards C#. I normally place my thumb on the top of the fretboard to provide leverage and support.

Adding bends to the b3 helps us catch a glimpse of the blues guitar sound. Don't worry too much if you don't manage to bend all the way to C#. Often we won't push the C all the way to C# anyway. A lot of fun can be had seeing how many different microtones we can find between the b3 and major 3.

Listen carefully to **exercise 1j** which demonstrates the minor 3rd being bent all the way up to the major 3rd.

Example 1j:

Now compare example 1i with example 1k where we don't necessarily make it all the way to C#.

It is good to be aware that we can just give the minor 3rd a little nudge towards major 3rd territory. When we bend a note slightly in this way it is called a curl."

This kind of bend quickly becomes natural and you will often find yourself unconsciously giving the C a little curl towards the C#.

In the following examples we will not be using curls, we will be playing the actual C# note over the A7 and moving it down by step to the C Natural on the D7. This is so you can easily hear the strength of the melodic movement. Later you may wish to explore this same idea but using bends and curls instead.

Here is a simple lick that demonstrates the major 3rd of A7 falling to the b7 of D7.

Example 1l:

You may feel that the strength of the melodic movement when targeting the b7 is a subtler than when we targeted the 3rd. This is because you will have already heard the b7 note (C) in the solo before, as it is contained in the A Minor Pentatonic scale.

When we targeted the 3rd of D7 (F#) we introduced a completely new note to the melody so it had a little more shock value.

These target notes sound even more subtle if they're contained within a complete line or lick. Here are a few that move from A7 to D7 to get you started.

Example 1m:

Example 1n:

In the next example I do not approach the C natural from C# to show that as long as the C natural is one of the first notes you play in the new bar, you will always get the effect of articulating the chord change.

Example 1o:

You don't have to hit the guide tone on beat one of the bar, so don't forget to experiment by leaving space at the beginning of the bar.

Now you have this sound in your head learn to play it in other octaves.

In this position, there are two more locations where you can target the b7 of the D7 chord: on the 1st string and on the 5th string. Here are some lines to help you get to grips with these positions.

Example 1p:

Targeting the b7 of D7 in the higher octave.

Example 1q:

Targeting the b7 of D7 in the lower octave.

Come up with your own lines with each of the target notes.

Chapter Two: Outlining the Chord IV to Chord I Movement

We have learned that as we move from chord I to chord IV, *the 3rd of chord I (A7) can always fall by a semitone to the b7 of chord IV*, and that the b7 of chord I will always fall by a semitone to the 3rd of chord IV.

In very simple terms, we can target the changing note on each chord change to align our solo with the harmony. By outlining this movement in our solo, we add interest and emotion to our solos.

When the chord changes from D7 back to A7 in bar 7 of the blues, we can use the same technique to outline the A7 chord by reversing the process.

When changing from D7 back to A7 (chord IV back to chord I)

1) The 3rd of Chord IV (D7) rises by a semitone to become the b7 of A7

2) The b7 of D7 rises by a semitone to become the 3rd of A7.

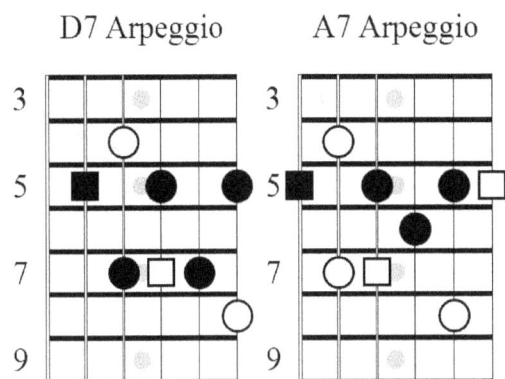

The 3rd of D7 (F#) is located on the 4th string, 4th fret (and on the 2nd string 7th fret).

The b7 of D7 (C) is located on 3rd string, 5th fret (and on the 1st string 8th fret).

The following example demonstrates the movement from the b7 of D7 to the 3rd of A7:

Example 2a:

The next lick highlights a typical line that uses the A Minor Pentatonic scale on the D7 chord then targets the 3rd of the A7 chord. All the lines in the chapter can be practised along with Backing Track 2.

Example 2b:

Example 2b is a similar idea, but this time bounces off the 3rd of A7 to create a bit of forward movement in the solo.

Example 2c:

Instead of overtly landing on the major 3rd of the A7 chord, we can target the chord change with a bend for a subtler approach.

Example 2d:

The next line adds a forward motion to the solo by using a combination of the targeted 3rd (C#) and the A Minor Pentatonic scale. Notice how I slide into the lower octave of the 3rd on the final note (5th string, 4th fret).

Example 2e:

When you have the sound of these lines in your ears, try targeting C#s on the A7 chord in the lower and higher octaves. You can do this on the 5th and 1st strings.

Now let's target the b7 of the A7 (G) as the chords change. This is a great effect but a little gentler because you will have already heard the b7 note in the previous bar. Also, the b7 guide tone isn't quite as strong as the 3rd in defining the chord sound.

In example 2f I approach the major 3rd of the D7 chord on beat 4 and then hit the b7 of A7 on beat one of the second bar. The line continues and targets the 3rd of A7 with a semitone bend before resting on the root.

Example 2f:

Example 2g targets the b7 of the A7 chord in the higher octave on the 2nd string. The final note of bar one is the 3rd of D7 which resolves up by step into the b7 of A7.

Example 2g:

Example 2h is a repeating figure that targets the 3rd of D7 with bends in bar one before hitting the higher octave of the b7 note in bar two.

Example 2h:

Example 2i is a little jazzier and includes a leap from the b7 to the 3rd on A7.

Example 2i:

Example 2j begins with a bend using the D *Mixolydian* mode and targets the b7 of A7 with another bend from the 3rd of D7 in the higher octave. We will discuss the Mixolydian mode in a later chapter.

Example 2j:

As always, these ideas are just here to give you an idea of what is possible with target notes. You will get the most immediate musical benefit by memorising a few of these ideas and then incorporating them into your own spontaneous improvisations.

Bring these ideas into your playing while jamming with Backing Track 1. When you have learned the movement on the fretboard, forget the theory and think about these lines as shapes and sounds.

Play these ideas in other keys. Try moving these licks to the keys of E, C and G.

Chapter Three: Outlining the Chord I to Chord V Movement

Chord V (E7 in the key of A) is the strongest chord in the 12-bar blues progression. This is where all the tension in the sequence occurs so targeting the chord change here is one of the most effective ways to add power and interest to your blues solo.

There are many ways to articulate the all-important V chord. Different scale choices are discussed in part two of this book, but for now we will focus on targeting the chord tones of the E7 chord to outline this important harmonic change.

There are two methods we can use to target the chord change.

1) Stay in the same fretboard position and introduce a new arpeggio shape

2) Change fretboard position and translate the arpeggio pattern from D7 up a tone.

While option two is certainly easier, option one more clearly demonstrates how the target notes change between A7 and E7.

Here are the chord shapes of A7 and E7 written out next to the A Minor Pentatonic scale:

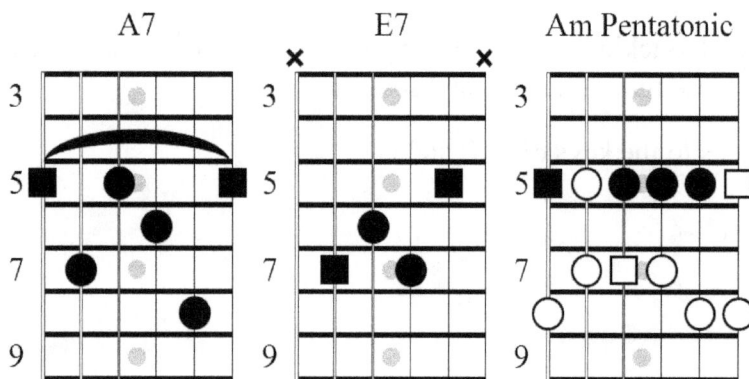

It is easy to see that a new note has been introduced. This note is the 3rd of the E7 chord (G#) and it is located on the 4th string, 6th fret. The higher octave of this note is played on the 1st string, 4th fret.

There is another new note introduced on chord change, but it isn't shown in this voicing of the E7 chord. It can be seen more easily when we compare the full *arpeggios* of each chord:

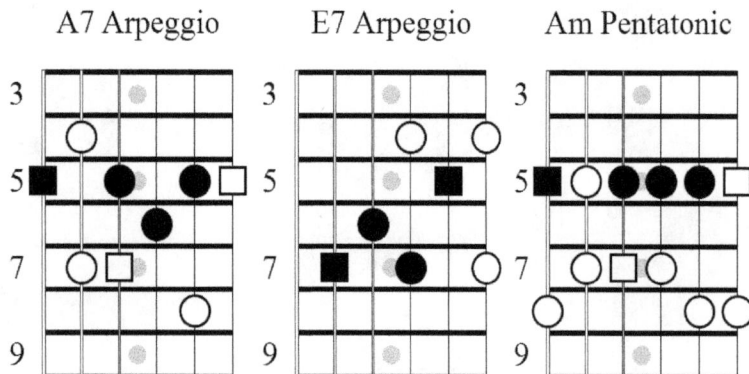

You can see that the new note introduced is the note 'B' played on the 3rd string, 4th fret, and the 1st string, 7th fret. When you compare the E7 arpeggio to the notes in the A7 arpeggio and the A Minor Pentatonic scale, you will see that this note has not been played before.

The note B is the 5th of the E7 chord, and while it is not strictly a guide tone, the fact that this note has not been targeted before in our solo makes it a strong note to play over the E7 chord.

We could target the b7 of the E7 chord (D). However, as D is the root of the *D7* chord it can sometimes sound a bit weak in this context.

The following lines for the A7 to E7 chord movement both target the 3rd of the E7 chord.

Example 3a:

The next lick targets the 3rd of E7 (G#) in the higher octave and then carries a bit more momentum through the chord change.

Example 3b:

You can practise all the ideas in this chapter over Backing Track 3, a cycle of A7 to E7.

Using more interesting rhythms helps add a bit of subtlety to the line:

Example 3c:

Example 3d:

Example 3e adds a bluesy bend to the line on the E7 chord.

Example 3e:

The following examples target the 5th (B) of the E7 chord.

Example 3f:

Example 3g combines the E7 arpeggio with the E Mixolydian scale and A Minor Pentatonic scale in bar two.

Example 3g:

Next, after targeting the B of the E7 chord, the E7 sound is reinforced by descending through the full E7 arpeggio.

Example 3h:

By thinking about chords individually you play notes you may not have considered with a purely Minor Pentatonic approach.

At every other point in the 12-bar blues progression, the bent note in bar two of example 3i will sound awful. By playing it at exactly the right time (targeting the 3rd of the E7 chord) we can add exciting melodic interest and surprise to our solo.

Example 3i:

Again in example 3j there is a bent note that might sound bad at other points in the progression. This time I'm bending from the b5 to the 5 on the E7.

Example 3j:

The following examples target the b7 (D) of the E7 chord.

Targeting the D on the E7 chord can sometimes be a little weak because it is the root note of the following chord in the 12-bar blues sequence (D7). To emphasise the change, I often play a C# note on the A chord (the 3rd) which the listener will hear moving to the D. This works better in higher octaves.

Example 3k:

Example 3l:

Example 3m:

The preceding ideas are useful for targeting the strongest notes on the E7 chord change, but there is another great way to recycle melodic material you already know. You can use the ideas we had for the IV chord (D7) and simply shift them up one tone to E7.

This can be seen clearly when we compare the chord diagrams for E7 and D7:

The following lines show how to change position on the guitar neck while easily outlining the E7 chord in a similar way to how we outlined the IV chord (D7) earlier.

Example 3n:

Example 3o:

Example 3p:

This technique comes into its own when we play the change from V to IV (E7 to D7) in bars 9 - 10 because we can easily take an E7 lick and move it down two frets (one tone) to become a D7 line. We can even get clever and add in some chromatic movement between the chords.

Chapter Four: Outlining the Chord V to Chord IV Movement

The movement between chord V (E7) and chord IV (D7) is the strongest harmonic point in the blues progression. The V chord descends by one tone to become the IV and this movement can be outlined easily in a solo with using guide tones and sequences.

We will begin by looking at some solo lines that approach playing the V to IV chord change using the same arpeggio shape and move it down the fretboard as the chord changes from E7 to D7.

When we change positions like this, it is easy to build strong melodic sequences with repeating phrases and patterns.

The following ideas move between the V and IV chords by sliding down the guitar neck and can be practised with Backing Track 4.

Example 4a:

Example 4b:

Example 4c:

Example 4d:

The chord change from V to IV normally only occurs once in a blues chord progression so these ideas can be tricky to practise. To help you practise, Backing Track 8 is a repeating chord sequence of this section which will help you to work specifically on this part of the blues form. The chords are as follows:

Practise playing these lines with Backing Track 8 and experimenting with different resolutions from the IV chord (D7) to the I chord (A7).

Write your own licks that outline the E7 and D7 chords using the previous examples as a guide.

Using shifting shapes in this way is useful for building sequential ideas. Stevie Ray Vaughan used this technique a lot. However, it is also important to master these chord changes without moving your hand around on the neck.

Let's look at how the chords of E7 and D7 can be played in the same position on the neck.

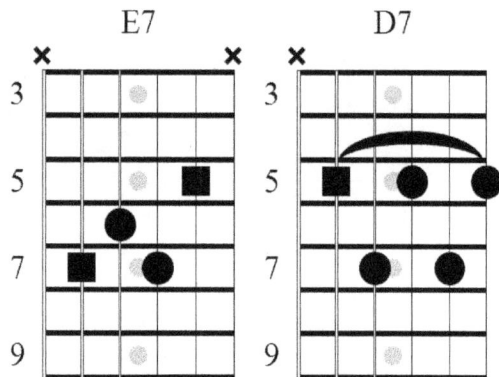

One of the important note-changes between these two chords can be seen clearly from just the chord diagrams. The 3rd of E7 (G#) rises by a semitone to become the 5th (A) of the D7 chord.

This shows that even though the chords may descend harmonically, intervals may still ascend between chords. It is an effective tool to use when you want your melodic line to go in the opposite direction to the bass movement of the chord change.

To see how the other important target notes change we need to take a deeper look at the full arpeggios of each chord:

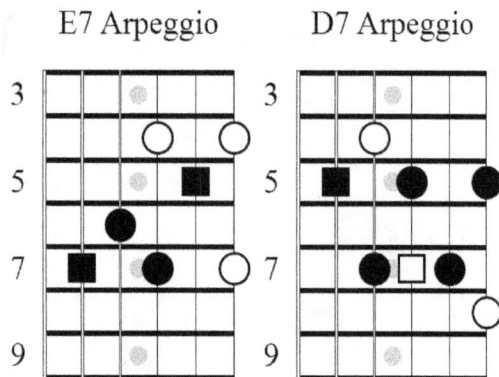

On the 3rd string, 4th fret you can see that the 5th of the E7 (B) chord rises by one semitone to become the b7 of the D7 chord (C).

The root of the E chord (E) on the 2nd string, 5th fret can move in one of two ways.

It can be seen as descending one tone to become the root of the D7 chord.

It can be seen as *ascending* one tone to become the 3rd of the D7 chord (F#). The latter much more interesting because it is in contrary motion to the bass movement.

The following examples highlight each target note in turn, and teach you lines that emphasise the strengths of each particular choice.

Targeting the 3rd of D7 (F#)

Example 4e emphasises the D7 sound with a line based around the arpeggio in bar two.

Example 4e:

Example 4f once targets the F# and uses the A Minor Pentatonic scale in bar two.

Example 4f:

Example 4g uses a chromatic approach (passing) note to target the F# on the D7 chord.

Example 4g:

In example 4h these is a descending passing note into the lower octave F# on the D7 chord.

Example 4h:

Targeting the 5th of D7 (A)

In example 4i, I target the 5th of the D7 chord with another chromatic approach note.

Example 4i:

Next, the A Minor Pentatonic scale is used over the E7 chord. However, the note G is bent up a semitone to target the 3rd of E7 (G#). The 5th is once again targeted on the D7 chord, however, the b3rd (F) is bent up by a semitone to hit the major 3rd (F#) for a slightly country sound.

Example 4j:

Here's a simple arpeggio idea over the E7 chord.

Example 4k:

Targeting the b7 of D7 (C)

This is a rhythmically simple line that targets the b7 of D7 (C).

Example 4l:

The following idea targets the b7 of the D7 chord in the higher octave.

Example 4m:

Example 4n first targets the b7 of D7 and then the 3rd on beat two.

Example 4n:

Finally, example 4o is a busier line with powerful forward motion.

Example 4o:

The approaches in the previous four chapters teach you to highligh a chord change by aiming for the strong guide tones of the new chord, or by hitting an arpeggio note on the change.

The method I encourage you to pursue is as follows.

1) Compare the two chord diagrams to see if any obvious notes are changing

2) Write out the arpeggios for each chord and look to see how the guide tones (3rds and 7ths) move.

3) Finally, check to see if other arpeggio notes (the root or 5th) provide a strong movement or can introduce new notes into the solo.

With this process, you will always be able to find interesting, emotive and unexpected notes to play in your solo. These will grab your audience's attention and keep them musically connected to your solo.

Finally, a 'pro tip'! A wonderful musical effect to exploit is to *bend* into the new target note. For example, instead of playing a line from A7 to D7 like this:

Example 4p:

Why not try it like this?

Example 4q:

Using a bend to target notes can really add something magical.

Also, by *delaying* the point at which you hit the target note, you can have a huge effect upon the listener.

Experiment with all the displacement ideas and techniques from **The Complete Guide to Blues Guitar Book Two: Melodic Phrasing.**

Here is one idea based around the previous lick to start you off.

Example 4r:

By simply adding a rest at the start of bar two, the delayed resolution adds surprise and feeling to your solo. Don't forget to add slides, bends and vibrato to each and every phrase.

Chapter Five: Chord Changes and Arpeggios in Every Position

All the ideas in the book so far have all been based around the 5th fret area of the guitar. This has been to stay focused on the concept of targeting arpeggio notes in your solos. However, only being able to play these changes in one position of the guitar neck is limiting in terms of range and expression.

The following pages provide chord diagrams and arpeggios for the chord changes of a 12-bar blues in A in each of the five positions on the neck. The 3rds and 7ths are marked to show you how the main target notes are moving.

Read the following diagrams from left to right to see how each important arpeggio note changes between chords I, IV and V in the Key of A. This will teach you how to target the closest note changes between each chord.

You will find many guide tone movements between chords and by incorporating these movements into your solos when the chords change, you will quickly develop an articulate and melodic approach to the blues.

Position One:

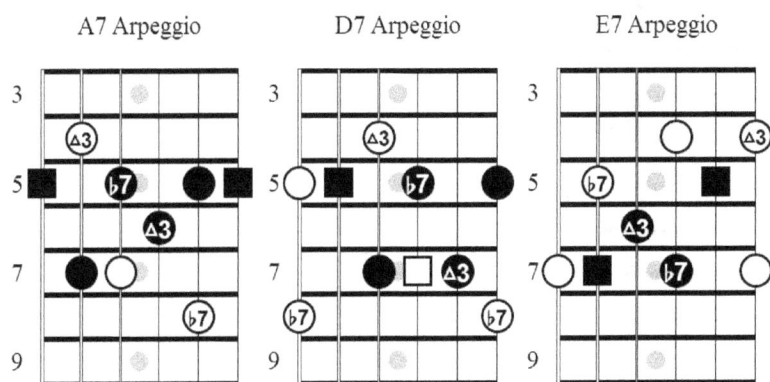

A7 Arpeggio   D7 Arpeggio   E7 Arpeggio

Position Two:

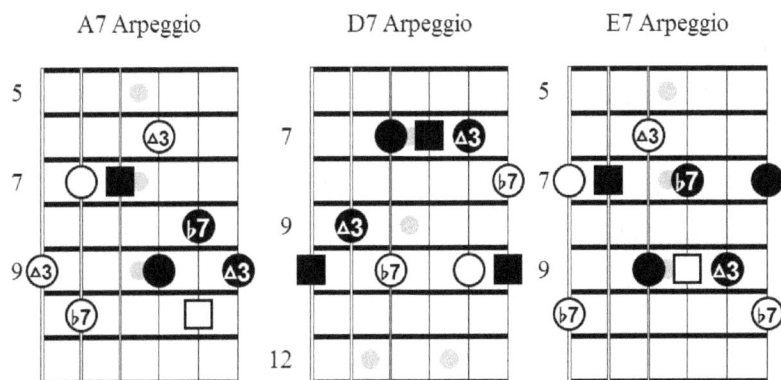

A7 Arpeggio   D7 Arpeggio   E7 Arpeggio

Position Three:

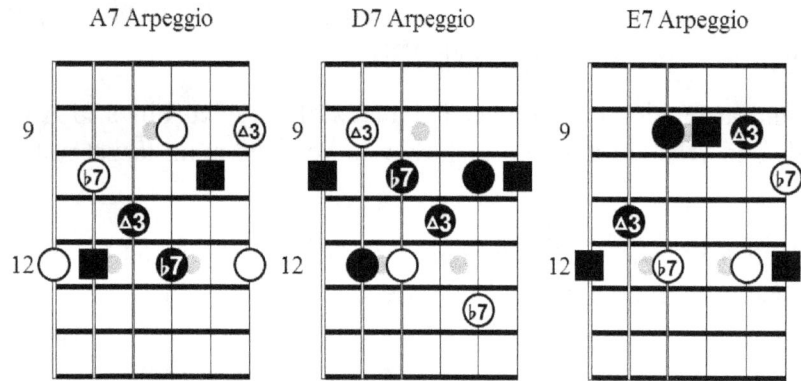

A7 Arpeggio   D7 Arpeggio   E7 Arpeggio

Position Four:

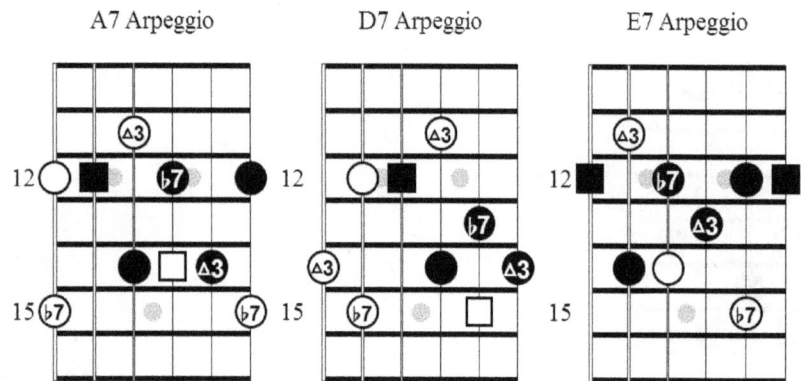

A7 Arpeggio   D7 Arpeggio   E7 Arpeggio

Position Five:

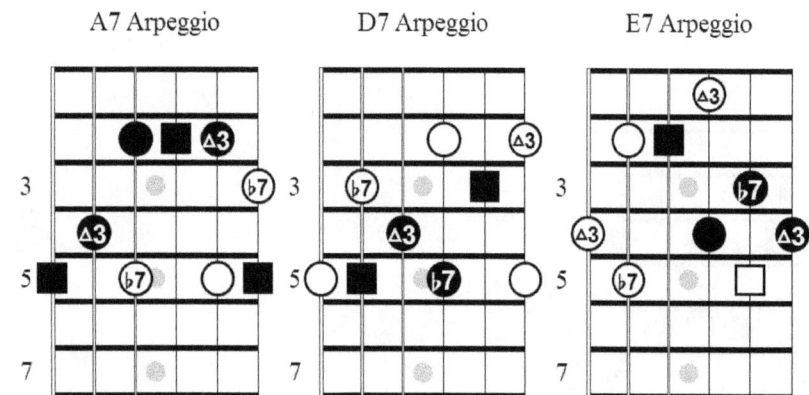

A7 Arpeggio   D7 Arpeggio   E7 Arpeggio

There are also some useful arpeggio exercises you can practise to reinforce the sounds and locations of the moving notes.

Practise the following exercises with Backing Track 9, a repeating chord sequence of:

Pick one area of the guitar neck from the diagrams above. In the following examples I use position three.

1) Play each arpeggio ascending from the root with four notes per bar:

Repeat the exercise descending from the higher root.

2) Play each arpeggio ascending from the 3rd:

Repeat the exercise descending from the higher octave 3rd.

3) Repeat the previous exercise beginning from the 5th and the b7th of each chord.

4) Now ascend the first arpeggio from the root but *target the closest note in the next chord* when the chords change:

You can travel in any direction or form patterns just so long as you hit a new arpeggio note on every change.

See how long you can keep playing this exercise without a mistake and fully explore each position.

5) Repeat the previous exercise but begin from the 3rd, 5th or b7 of the A7 chord.

6) Limit your playing to just two or three strings and play the same exercises:

7) Play all the above exercises in 1/8th notes instead of 1/4 notes.

8) Finally, combine these exercises with short A Minor Pentatonic ideas and target arpeggio notes when the chords change for a much more bluesy, musical approach:

Repeat these exercises in every position and soon you will be able to see, feel and hear the arpeggio changes without having to think about them.

As you can see in the final example, these arpeggio exercises really come alive when the target notes are mixed with Minor Pentatonic licks. Working regularly on the previous eight exercises will improve your playing very quickly.

Part Two - Scales and Soloing Schemes

Chapter Six: Scale Choices for the I Chord

i. The Major Pentatonic Scale

Part one of this book dealt with the concept of articulating a chord change with the notes in our solo. We found that by targeting particular notes from a chord or arpeggio we were able to introduce new, appropriate sounds into our melodies and add interest and feeling to our playing.

However, once we have used a target note to 'play our way' into the new chord, there are often many scale options that can be used to continue the solo. Different scales have different feelings or *colours* and by mastering their different sounds we can manipulate our audiences' emotions to take them on a journey throughout the solo.

Eventually, these sounds will become second nature to you, and you won't think about scales at all when you solo; just moods and expression. However, to begin with, it is important to learn, understand and hear how each scale functions and feels.

After the Minor Pentatonic, the next most common scale choice to use on the I chord (A7) is the *Major Pentatonic* scale.

You may already be aware of this scale and know the easy 'trick' to play it on the guitar. To play an A Major Pentatonic scale simply move an A Minor Pentatonic scale down three frets. For example, here is one way to play the A Major Pentatonic scale:

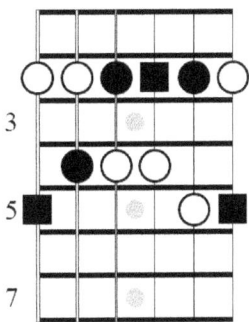

A Major Pentatonic

You can see that on paper, this looks very much like the scale of F# Minor Pentatonic, but because we hear it over an A major chord we hear the intervals of the scale in relation to the root note A.

Another way to see that this is an A Major Pentatonic scale is by looking at the location of the root notes (the square dots) of the scale. The root note is on the 5th fret of the 6th string (A) and not on the F# (2nd fret).

Try improvising a solo with the A Major Pentatonic scale over the blues progression in Backing Track 5. It sounds great over the A7 chords but doesn't fit so well over the D7 chords.

If you struggle to get started it can help to take an A Minor Pentatonic lick that you know and simple move it down three frets like this:

Example 6a:

Here are some useful A Major Pentatonic licks that use this scale shape.

Example 6b:

Example 6c:

Example 6d:

Even with just these few examples and improvising your own Major Pentatonic lines you will quickly realise two things:

1) The A Major Pentatonic scale sounds much happier than the A Minor Pentatonic scale.

2) The A Major Pentatonic scale really doesn't sound that good when the chord changes to D7.

The Major Pentatonic scale sounds happier because it contains different notes to the A Minor Pentatonic scale.

The notes in A Minor Pentatonic are

A C D E and G (formula 1 b3 4 5 b7)

In A Major Pentatonic the notes are

A B C# E and F# (formula 1 2 3 5 6)

By staying away from the b3 and adding the 6th our brain perceives the Major Pentatonic as a happier sound.

The reason that the A Major Pentatonic scale doesn't work well over the D7 chord is because A Major Pentatonic contains the note C#. This C# clashes heavily with the important b7 chord tone C in the D7 chord.

As C (b7) is one of the most important notes in the D7 chord, a C# will introduce a strong, undesired dissonance to the melody.

The solution is to = use a different scale when the chord changes to D7, but we will look at that later.

Moving the A Minor Pentatonic scale down three frets to create an A Major Pentatonic scale is a useful trick, but we don't always want to be *forced* into a specific position on the neck. For this reason, it is beneficial to learn the A Major Pentatonic scale at the fifth fret so it's easy to move between the A Minor and A Major Pentatonic scales in one position.

Here is how to play the A Major Pentatonic scale at the fifth fret:

A Major Pentatonic
Shape 1

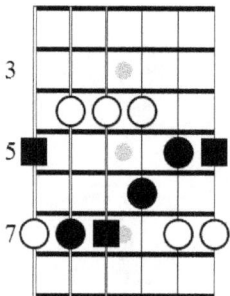

This scale shape may be slightly unfamiliar to you, so learn it ascending and descending until you have it memorised. Don't worry too much about specific fingerings although I normally like to begin with my second finger on the lowest note.

Here are some useful licks based around this pattern of the A Major Pentatonic scale:

Example 6e:

Example 6f:

Example 6g:

Example 6h:

Now learn the Major Pentatonic scale all over the neck in the key of A and try to improvise some solos with it.

Here are the five shapes you need to know:

A Major Pentatonic Shape 1	A Major Pentatonic Shape 2	A Major Pentatonic Shape 3	A Major Pentatonic Shape 4	A Major Pentatonic Shape 5

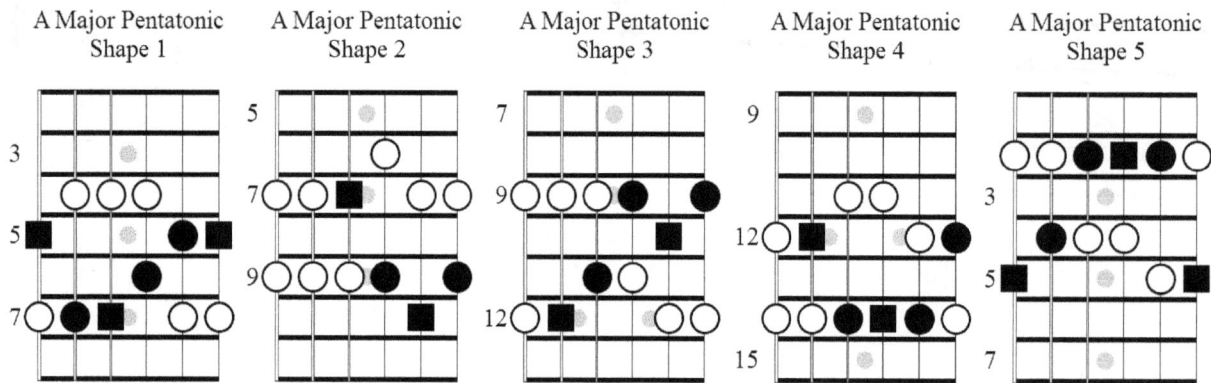

For more Major Pentatonic ideas and a complete guide to the CAGED System, check out my bestselling book **The CAGED System and 100 Licks for Blues Guitar.**

ii. The Blues scale

The Blues scale is interchangeable with the Minor Pentatonic scale. They are identical except for the addition of one note, the 'b5' in the Blues scale.

The Minor Pentatonic scale has the formula

1 b3 4 5 b7

The Blues scale has the formula

1 b3 4 b5 5 b7

Here are the fretboard diagrams of both scales:

Am Pentatonic   Am Pentatonic

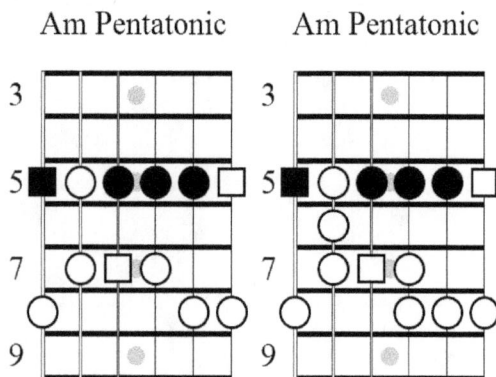

The addition of this single note makes a marked difference to the sound of the melody solos.

A great way to hear how this extra note makes a huge difference to your playing is to begin by altering some Minor Pentatonic licks that you already know. Take this line for example:

Example 6i:

By adding in the *blue note* we create a different sound:

Example 6j:

It is also common to bend from the 4th (D) to the b5th (Eb) like this:

Example 6k:

The b5 is also useful when played in the lower octave:

Example 6l:

Example 6m:

Here are some more useful licks formed from the Blues scale:

Example 6n:

Example 6o:

Example 6p:

Example 6q:

As always, you should practise improvising with the Blues scale all over the neck.

Here are the five scale patterns you need to know.

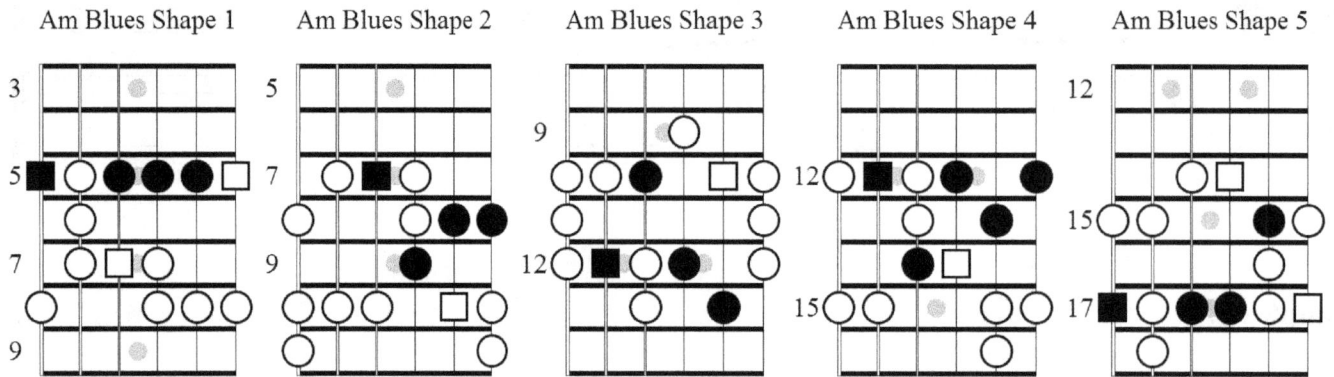

| Am Blues Shape 1 | Am Blues Shape 2 | Am Blues Shape 3 | Am Blues Shape 4 | Am Blues Shape 5 |

iii. The Mixolydian Mode

A common and important scale choice on the I chord is the scale of A Mixolydian.

Mixolydian is the fifth *mode* of the Major scale and contains all the notes from the A7 arpeggio plus the notes from the A Major Pentatonic scale.

As a formula it is written: 1 2 3 4 5 6 b7

In the key of A the notes are A B C# D E F# G

As you can see, it contains the intervals from A dominant 7 arpeggio:

1 3 5 b7

A C# E G

and the notes from the Major Pentatonic scale

1 2 3 5 6

A B C# E F#

It also includes the 4th from the Minor Pentatonic scale (D)

As the Mixolydian sound is close to the chord arpeggio, the Mixolydian scale is almost always combined with the Minor Pentatonic and Blues scales to give it a little bit of bite, character and aggression.

The scale of A Mixolydian is played in the following way. I have included a diagram of the A Blues scale next to the diagram of the Mixolydian mode to help you see how these scales can be combined. It is useful to see the similarities and differences between the two because Mixolydian is almost always combined with the Minor Pentatonic scale.

A Mixolydian Shape 1   Am Blues Shape 1

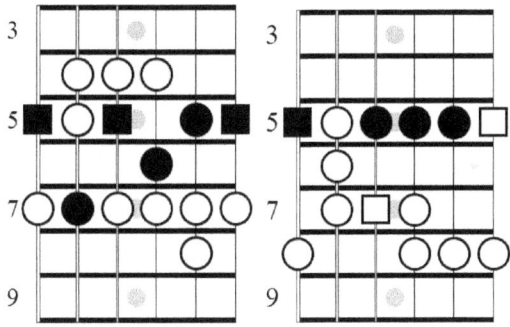

Try playing the Mixolydian scale ascending and descending over the A7 chords in Backing Track 1. It almost sounds a bit too 'correct'.

It is easy to hear that the notes are correct but it doesn't sound very bluesy. When I use the Mixolydian mode in a blues solo I tend to think of the Minor Pentatonic/Blues scale as a framework and stir in some notes of the Mixolydian mode for a brighter colour. It's almost like playing a combination of Minor and Major Pentatonic scales played at the same time.

The following licks are created by combining the A Mixolydian and A Minor Pentatonic/Blues scales.

Example 6r:

Example 6s:

Example 6t:

Example 6u:

Example 6v:

Study the previous examples carefully. Can you see how elements of both the Minor Pentatonic scale and the Mixolydian mode are combined freely to create an authentic blues sound?

These examples are just the tip of the iceberg. One musical way to practise this concept is to look for notes that are contained in the Mixolydian mode but not in the Minor Pentatonic scale. Try bending or sliding from Mixolydian notes into Minor Pentatonic notes and vice versa.

For example, instead of this standard Minor Pentatonic line:

Example 6w:

Convert it into a brighter sounding Mixolydian lick:

Example 6x:

The previous two ideas work on the 1st string too.

There are plenty of opportunities for this kind of conversion and you should practise this concept all over the next. Here is the scale of A Mixolydian in the five main fretboard positions. Each is shown next to its related Blues scale.

A Mixolydian Shape 1   Am Blues Shape 1

A Mixolydian Shape 2   Am Blues Shape 2

A Mixolydian Shape 3   **Am Blues Shape 3**

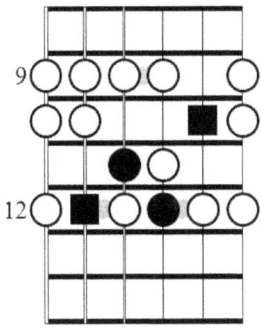

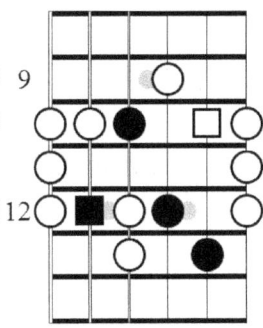

A Mixolydian Shape 4   **Am Blues Shape 4**

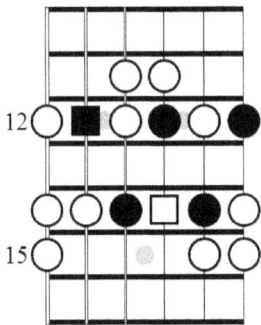

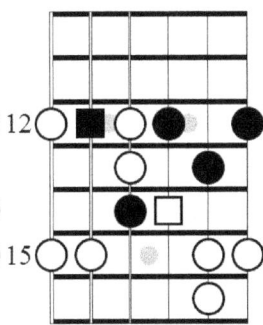

A Mixolydian Shape 5   **Am Blues Shape 5**

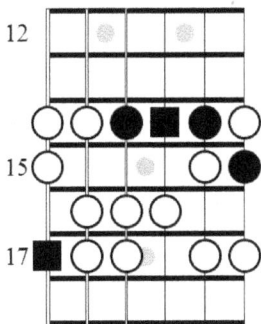

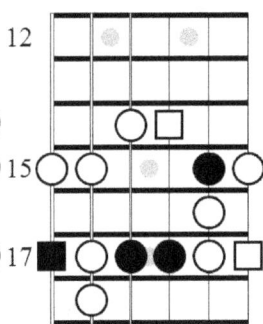

You may have already guessed that you can use the D Mixolydian mode on the D7 (IV) chord and E Mixolydian on the E7 (V) chord. We will look at this in more detail later.

Chapter Seven: Scale Choices for the IV Chord

i. The Tonic Minor Pentatonic on Chord IV

As we learned in Chapter Six, the tonic A Major Pentatonic scale sounds dissonant against the IV (D7) chord. This means that we need to change scale when the harmony changes to D7. There are a few options to use, but my favourite choice is to play the A Minor Pentatonic scale over the D7 chord.

One reason for this is that the A Minor Pentatonic scale contains the b7 note of D7 (C). We can, therefore, use the A Minor Pentatonic to target this note. If we have previously used the A Major Pentatonic scale to solo over the A7 chord, then the note C will not have been played until this point, and its introduction is a nice surprise on the chord change.

It is important to notice that the A Minor Pentatonic scale (A C D E G) does *not* include the important 3rd of the D chord (F#) so it is acceptable to add it in whenever we like.

Here is a simple line that uses the A Major Pentatonic scale on the A7 chord and moves to A Minor Pentatonic on the D7 chord. The line targets the b7 of D7 (C) on the chord change.

I play A Major Pentatonic at the second fret and slide the scale up three frets to play A Minor Pentatonic.

Example 7a:

Here are a couple of ideas that change between the A Major Pentatonic and A Minor Pentatonic scales while staying at the fifth fret:

Example 7b:

Example 7c:

Let's not forget all the work we did in Chapter One. We can still target the major 3rd of the D7 chord (F#) when the chord changes (even though it is not in the A Minor Pentatonic scale), and then continue the line with the A Minor Pentatonic scale.

Example 7d:

Example 7e:

The key is lots of experimentation and jamming. Remember, just because a scale option is available, you don't have to play it. This is a mistake I often used to make; I'd try to cram in every possible piece of theory into one bar, when in fact a great way to play is to suggest a scale as subtly as possible.

Another important consideration is deciding *when* you're going to play, not *what* you're going to play. By thinking of rhythm and note placement, you take instant command over your solo.

Aim to start your D7 line at a specific point in the bar, for example in the middle of beat three:

Example 7f:

By using this much space between my lines, I effectively highlight the difference in scale choice between bars one and two. I still use A Major Pentatonic in bar one and A Minor Pentatonic in bar two, but by picking the specific point where I will place my notes I give myself room to build my solo and the audience time to appreciate each phrase.

ii. Minor Pentatonic on the IV Chord

As we used the A Major Pentatonic scale over the chord of A7 it may seem obvious to play the D Major Pentatonic scale over the D7 chord. However, This is actually a bit of a musical grey area.

In theory, the scale should work well but in my opinion the D Major Pentatonic scale isn't a great choice for the D7 chord, although you should definitely test this out for yourself.

The D Major Pentatonic does not contain the b7 of the D chord (C) which feels like a powerful note at this point in the progression. Its omission really detracts from the classic blues sound. You'll remember from Chapter One that the movement from the 3rd of A7 (C#) to the b7 of the D7 (C) is one of the defining characteristics and important sounds in the blues.

By playing a D Major Pentatonic scale at this point we lose the opportunity to exploit this movement.

Of course, you could play a D Major Pentatonic scale and add in the b7 (C) note, but this sound is so close to the Mixolydian scale that most people simply play Mixolydian instead.

A good choice for the D7 chord is the D Minor Pentatonic scale, though it tends to work best if we bend the b3 note (F) towards major territory (F#). We looked briefly at this idea earlier when we discussed bending into guide tones from a semitone below.

This is the fretboard diagram for D Minor Pentatonic at the 5th fret. The black note on the 2nd string is the minor 3rd that you'll want to bend towards the major 3rd.

Dm Pentatonic

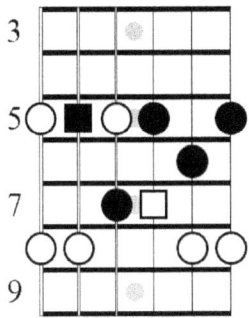

Here are some lines for the IV chord based around D Minor Pentatonic scale. Notice how I usually bend the F towards F#.

Example 7g:

Example 7h:

Example 7i:

Using a D Minor Pentatonic scale over the D7 chord is a common melodic technique but the b3 (F) does need to be handled with care. The most common way to deal with this note is to bend it up towards the major 3rd (F#) as I have shown.

iii. Mixolydian on the IV chord

Playing the Mixolydian mode on chord IV works much in the same way as playing the Mixolydian mode on chord I. It is a common approach because the Mixolydian scale contains all the notes from the dominant 7 chord plus some great-sounding colours.

Over the chord of D7 we can use the D Mixolydian mode. At the 5th fret, D Mixolydian can be played like this:

D Mixolydian Shape 4

The D Mixolydian mode is not related to the tonic key of A so it is used *only* over the D7 chord. When we play a different scale over each chord, we view each chord change as a temporary modulation (key change) to the tonality of D Mixolydian.

Using D Mixolydian over D7 is the same as using A Mixolydian on an A7 chord. The D Mixolydian mode contains all the chord tones of D7 (D, F#, A and C) plus all the notes from D Major Pentatonic (D, E, F#, A and B). It also contains the 4th interval from the D Minor Pentatonic scale, (G).

Once again, it is normally combined with the D Minor Pentatonic/Blues scale, however, once again, the minor 3rd is often bent up towards the major 3rd.

Before learning new vocabulary based around the above shape of D Mixolydian, let's look at an easy way to recycle some of the Mixolydian lines we used on the A7 chord.

The easiest way to access the Mixolydian sound on D7 is to slide an A Mixolydian lick you already know up by five frets. Just as if we were moving a barre chord up the neck from A7 to D7.

For example, Here's the lick from example 6r:

To play it as a D Mixolydian lick, slide it up five frets. Stevie Ray Vaughan was a huge fan of this technique.

Example 7j:

Here is the A Mixolydian from example 6s:

And here it is moved up five frets the neck to become a D Mixolydian line:

Example 7k:

Learning to move lines around the neck into new keys is an essential part of learning the guitar, so try playing all your licks in different keys.

Moving the scale shape up and down the neck is useful, but it is also important to be able to change keys while staying in the same position.

The following lines are based around the D Mixolydian scale shape shown at the beginning of this section. The root note, D is on the 5th string, 5th fret.

These examples all begin on an arpeggio tone of D7, They then continue by using a combination of the D Mixolydian and D Minor Pentatonic scales. I often bend into the arpeggio tone from a semitone below for a more bluesy effect.

Example 7l:

Example 7m:

Example 7n

Example 7o

Example 7p:

Example 7q:

Chapter Eight: Scale Choices for the V Chord

i. The Tonic Minor Pentatonic on Chord V

There are many possible scale choices for the V (E7) chord, and one of the most common sounds is to use the Minor Pentatonic scale played from the key of the song. In our case this is A Minor Pentatonic. We have covered this scale in great depth already.

There is however, a danger in blanketing the blues progression with the tonic Minor Pentatonic scale. By doing so, it is easy to lose sight and sound of the harmonic subtleties that occur when the chords change and that we aim to bring out with intelligent scale choice.

This book has been all about enhancing and articulating these harmonic movements by careful choice of arpeggio notes and guide tones, so in this section we will study a small change we can make to one note of the A Minor Pentatonic scale to make it perfectly outline the E7 chord.

You may remember that one of the strongest notes to target in the E7 chord is the 3rd (G#). The A Minor Pentatonic scale does *not* contain this note but there is a simple way to include it. All we need to do is alter one of the most commonly bent notes in the scale.

When you solo with the A Minor Pentatonic scale you have probably played lines like this:

Example 8a:

The final note in the previous phrase is a whole tone bend from the note G to the note A. To target the G# note on an E7 chord we simply change this whole-tone bend into a half-tone bend. Instead of bending to G, we bend to G# instead.

This bend is particularly strong if played it right on the chord change:

Example 8b:

By altering just this one note, it is easy to use A Minor Pentatonic scale to outline the E7 sound. Remember though, the G# will sound terrible at any almost other point in the progression. It only works on the E7 chord.

Here are a couple of lines to get your started. Notice in example 8c how I repeat the G - G# bend in the lower octave.

Example 8c:

The C natural of the A Minor Pentatonic scale will normally need to be given a little curl towards C# territory as this it a slightly sweeter note against the E7 chord.

Example 8d:

Example 8e:

Example 8f:

ii. Minor Pentatonic on Chord V

Just as we used the D Minor Pentatonic scale over D7, we can also use the E Minor Pentatonic scale over E7. However, it is important to remember that we will nearly always bend the b3 (G) towards the major 3rd territory (G#).

A simple way to access this sound is to take any D Minor Pentatonic lick you know and move it up by a tone to work on the E7 chord. For example, here is a D Minor Pentatonic lick from example 7g.

Here it is shifted up a tone to become an E Minor Pentatonic lick:

Example 8g:

Remember, you can also move an A Minor Pentatonic / Blues scale lick up to the 12th fret area to create an E Minor Pentatonic lick. Let's try it with this example 6j.

Here is the same line shifted (transposed) up the neck to create an E7 line:

Example 8h:

These two techniques are very useful, but we should also learn some E Minor Pentatonic vocabulary at the 5th fret so we don't have to 'chase' licks around the fretboard.

Here's how to play the E Minor Pentatonic / Blues scale at the 5th - 7th fret:

Em Pentatonic Shape 3   Em Blues Shape 3

An advantage of using E Minor Pentatonic as opposed to A Minor Pentatonic over the E7 chord is that it contains the 5th of the E7 chord. As we learned earlier, this is an extremely powerful target note as it only occurs in the E7 chord.

The following lines demonstrate how to use the E Minor Pentatonic scale over the E7 chord. Notice that the b3 (G) is normally bent towards the major 3rd (G#) if it occurs at a rhythmically strong point in the bar.

Example 8i:

Example 8j:

Example 8k:

Don't forget, any of these lines can be played a tone (two frets) lower as a D7 lick.

iii. Minor Pentatonic on the 5th of the V Chord

Just as we used the A Minor Pentatonic to play over the D7 chord in Chapter Seven, it possible to use the *B Minor Pentatonic* to solo over the E7 chord.

Playing a Minor Pentatonic scale build from the fifth of the chord is a common technique that's used a lot in rock and explained in more detail in my book, **The Practical Guide to Modern Music Theory.**

The 5th of the E7 chord is the note B, so we can play B Minor Pentatonic over the E7 chord.

The quickest way to hear this relationship is to simply move an A Minor Pentatonic line that we played on the D7 chord up by one tone to become a B Minor Pentatonic line over the E7 chord.

For example, here is an A Minor Pentatonic line (example 7b).

This line uses the A Major Pentatonic scale on the A7 chord and switches to A Minor Pentatonic scale on the D7 chord.

Let's keep the first half of the line the same on the A7 chord, but shift the second half of the line up by a tone to suit an E7 chord:

Example 8l:

This is a common approach for the dominant chord in a blues. You do have to be a little careful, because the B Minor Pentatonic scale contains the note F# which is an important chord tone of the D7 chord. As we are soloing over an E7 chord I'll avoid hitting the F# note on the chord change as it can sound a bit ambiguous. Essentially, you're playing a strong major 3rd of the IV chord over the V chord.

Use Backing Track 10 to practise this concept, the chord progression on the backing track is:

Choose a single idea to play on the A7 chord and move it up a tone so it becomes a B Minor Pentatonic line over the E7 chord.

Use your ears to decide if the notes you are targeting work musically. Here are a few more B Minor Pentatonic lines for you to play on the E7 chord:

Example 8m:

Here I let the E7 chord settle before playing the line to enhance its strength.

Example 8n:

To play the B Minor Pentatonic scale in the same position as the other chords in the blues, it can be played like this:

Bm Pentatonic Shape 5

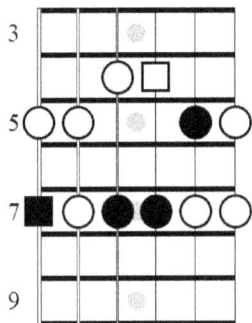

The following lines are based around this scale shape. I also freely add in the 3rd of the E7 chord (G#) to enhance the strength of the line.

Example 8o:

Example 8p:

Example 8q:

You may have noticed that playing the B Minor Pentatonic scale over the E7 is almost like playing the A Major Pentatonic scale over the E7 chord. In fact, there is only one note different between the two scales.

These subtle differences between scale choice become common when we look in so much detail at the soloing possibilities because only a certain amount of notes are be strongly related to the E7 sound.

Try this A Major Pentatonic line over the E7 chord:

Example 8r:

Whether you 'think' A Major Pentatonic or B Minor Pentatonic over the E7 chord will create subtle differences in the feel of your solo over the dominant chord. My advice is to experiment, pick your favourite and stick with it.

iv. Major Pentatonic on the V Chord

Using the Major Pentatonic scale on the V chord is another common choice. It can be a little bright for some people, maybe even a little country-sounding, but when combined with the Minor Pentatonic scale or other previously discussed ideas, it contains all the ingredients of an articulate solo over the Dominant V chord.

The big advantage to using E Major Pentatonic on E7 is that contains the major 3rd. The notes in the scale are:

E F# G# B and C#

These intervals are the root, 9th, 3rd 5th and 13th of the scale.

If you recap Chapter Four, you will see that the 3rd (G#) and the 5th (B) are both strong notes to target on the V (E7) chord.

Here is the scale diagram for E Major Pentatonic at the 12th fret:

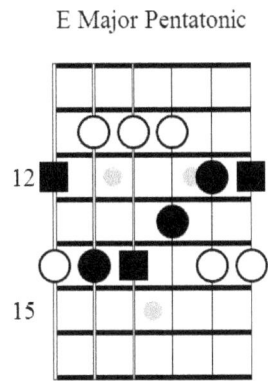

E Major Pentatonic

As always, the quickest way to access a new sound is to modify something you already know. Let's move an A Major Pentatonic lick up the neck and play it as an E Major Pentatonic lick. Here is example 6g.

To transpose this line into an E Major Pentatonic lick, move the shape up to the 12 fret like this:

Example 8s:

Try transposition with any A Major Pentatonic or D Major Pentatonic licks you learnt in previous chapters. By now you should be finding it easy to move Pentatonic licks into different keys.

To play the E Major Pentatonic scale close to the fifth fret you can use this scale shape:

E Major Pentatonic

Here are some lines based around this position. Again, I regularly combine notes from both the Major Pentatonic and Minor Pentatonic scales.

Example 8t:

Example 8u:

Example 8v:

v. Mixolydian on the V Chord

The final scale choice to explore is E Mixolydian Mode on the E7 chord. There are many similarities between the Mixolydian mode and the Major Pentatonic scale. However, the Mixolydian mode contains a few extra notes, notably a b7 guide tone that helps it fit perfectly around the V7 chord.

To quickly access the Mixolydian sound on the E7 chord, transpose some first position A Mixolydian lines up the neck to the 12th fret area. Try shifting this lick from example 6t:

Here is how to play that line with an E root.

Example 8w:

Try moving other A Mixolydian and D Mixolydian licks up the neck to the key of E to access instant vocabulary and get your ears used to this new sound.

The E Mixolydian mode can be played in the 5th-7th fret position in the following way:

E Mixolydian

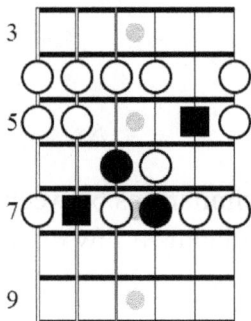

Here are some E Mixolydian licks based around the above scale shape. As always, I freely combine Minor Pentatonic and Blues scale notes into the lines.

Example 8x:

Example 8y:

Example 8z:

Mixolydian on the dominant chord is a favourite sound of many blues guitar players, but the best playing is normally a combination of many different approaches.

In the final chapter, we'll discuss how to practise these concepts efficiently and incorporate them into our playing. If we have a structured approach practice, then these ideas will quickly combine and become natural to us in our solos.

One important truth that many musicians miss is that all this study just boils down to ear training. Do you really want to be thinking scales when you're playing? Or do you want to simply hear and feel where the right notes are on the guitar?

The type of deep study in this book is an essential stage in your development as a musician. Without studying scale permutations and guide tones you will always be in a situation where 'you don't know what you don't know'. By studying the most important scale choices individually and simply working with the ones you like, you will always be in control of what you play. You will have taught your ears the possible sounds and you will develop a personal language by combining them.

Not every scale choice in this book will be to your taste. If you don't like something, do give it a chance and work with it for a while. However, if you still don't like it, simply disregard it and move on to something better.

Chapter 9: How to Practise

There is a vast amount of information in this book. It covers everything from targeting the defining notes of each chord, to multiple different scale choices for every chord in the blues. If you don't develop a structured approach to learning and assimilating all these sounds, then the task of learning all the permutations will feel overwhelming.

My first piece of advice is a warning: Try to avoid the thought, "But what if...?"

I will admit that I'm still guilty of this one, but I'm getting better. Sometimes I'll be soloing, creating melodies and trying to express myself on the guitar. I'll be playing over a blues or a jazz progression and letting my ears guide my playing. Then suddenly I get the thought, "But what if I was using a different scale? Would that sound better? Shouldn't I play *a clever* bit of theory just to show people how knowledgeable I am?"

Maybe you can relate to this. The more we study, the more soloing options we have, and the more we get affected by the thought, "But what if...?"

Unfortunately, at this point I've already lost the game because I've started to think about music theory, and not about playing music and melody.

The way to combat this is to realise that *everything* we practise is just ear training. The time for practising scales and theory is in the practice room. As soon as you sit down to play something meaningful you must switch off that internal dialogue that worries about what you're *not* playing.

You must focus on, and listen to the melody in your head and the notes coming from your guitar. Focus on the music and melody, and hear the next note that you'll play before you play it. If you've done the work in the practice room, the new concepts will eventually get into your ears and under your fingers. If you find it's not coming, practise more slowly. Sing every note before you play it and develop the connection between the brain and fingers.

If you're in any doubt leave silence until you hear the next melody in your head, and then play it. It's difficult at first but practise playing only what you hear inside you.

The quickest way to do this is to sing what you play. This might be embarrassing or awkward at first, but no one has to hear you. It's the one sure-fire way to connect the music inside you to your fingers and your guitar.

If you get stuck when you're on stage, pick one theoretical concept and make music from it. Remember, the most powerful tools you have at your disposal are rhythm, feel and placement. The simplest musical concept will sound incredible when played with impeccable feel.

Above all, switch off from "But what if...?" and focus on the music you're making in the moment.

You may feel that none of this is relevant to you, but in my experience, it has affected every musician I have spoken to. Almost without exception they have all said, "Leave space, keep it simple, and think rhythm."

Let's look at how to incorporate the scales in this book tangibly into our playing.

We have studied many possible scale choices for each chord of the blues progression.

Here they all are written out in the key of A:

Chord I: A7

- A Minor Pentatonic scale

- A Blues scale

- A Major Pentatonic scale

- A Mixolydian scale

Chord IV: D7

- D Minor Pentatonic scale

- A Minor Pentatonic scale

- D Mixolydian scale

- (D Major Pentatonic also possible)

Chord V: E7

- A Minor Pentatonic

- E Minor Pentatonic

- B Minor Pentatonic

- E Major Pentatonic

- E Mixolydian scale

Pick just one soloing approach for each chord. Always begin with your favourite (If you don't have a favourite yet pick one randomly).

Write out the 12-bar blues progression and write in the approach you'll use on each chord. Always use the same approach for the same chord type. For example, if you've decided to use Major Pentatonic on the A7 chord, A Minor Pentatonic on D7 and E Mixolydian on the E7 chords, *stick to it*!

Your soloing scheme will look something like this:

Keep this soloing scheme in front of you and do not deviate from your plan. If other ideas creep in then that's good in one sense, because your musical ear is taking over, but for right now the goal is to make sure that your practice is focused and disciplined.

You may wish to begin by writing out defined licks to play over each chord. This can help at first when it is challenging to improvise smoothly while changing scales over each chord. If you struggle, don't be afraid to use a very slow backing track or simply isolate each chord before putting everything back together.

It may take days, weeks, or months to become fully comfortable with a soloing choice, but if something really isn't working for you don't be afraid to disregard it and try something new. There's no point wasting your time trying to make something you don't like work when the perfect scale choice could be just around the corner!

When you you're starting to get to grips with your initial choices, replace your least favourite scale choice with a new one. If you like all the choices just randomly replace one with something else. For example, in the previous example, you could replace all the A Major Pentatonic scales with A Minor Pentatonic scales.

Next, spend time trying new licks and freely improvising with the scales. Experiment with the rhythmic concepts from **The Complete Guide to Blues Guitar Book Two: Melodic Phrasing** while staying within the chosen set scale choices. This is how you find your own voice and get inside the scale.

Every few weeks switch out one scale and try a new one. Before you know it, your ears and improvisational ability will improve dramatically.

Make a note of your favourite scales and develop your soloing with those. It could be that your favourites sounds are co-dependent. For example, you may only like the sound A Minor Pentatonic on the D7 chord if you played A Mixolydian on the A7. Make a note of these relationships and work on them in different positions on the guitar neck and in different keys. Begin by focusing on the keys of A, E, C and Bb.

Finally, listen!

Listen to the blues players you like. We are all products of who we listen to and how we practise. Treat listening as part of your practise routine. Put your guitar down and see if you can recognise the approaches your favourite musicians use. When you have listened to a tune a few times, pick up your guitar and try to copy short solo phrases like. B.B. King is great for this because he often leaves big gaps between short, uncomplicated phrases.

Keep it simple, have fun and enjoy the process of developing your musical ears.

Good luck,

Joseph

Be Social

Join over 10,000 people getting six free guitar lessons every day on Facebook:

www.facebook.com/FundamentalChangesInGuitar

Keep up to date on Twitter

@Guitar_Joseph

Other Books from Fundamental Changes

The Complete Guide to Playing Blues Guitar Book One: Rhythm Guitar

The Complete Guide to Playing Blues Guitar Book Two: Melodic Phrasing

The Complete Guide to Playing Blues Guitar Book Three: Beyond Pentatonics

The Complete Guide to Playing Blues Guitar Compilation

The CAGED System and 100 Licks for Blues Guitar

Minor ii V Mastery for Jazz Guitar

Jazz Blues Soloing for Guitar

Guitar Scales in Context

Guitar Chords in Context

The First 100 Chords for Guitar

Jazz Guitar Chord Mastery

Complete Technique for Modern Guitar

Funk Guitar Mastery

The Complete Technique, Theory & Scales Compilation for Guitar

Sight Reading Mastery for Guitar

Rock Guitar Un-CAGED

The Practical Guide to Modern Music Theory for Guitarists

Beginner's Guitar Lessons: The Essential Guide

Chord Tone Soloing for Jazz Guitar

Chord Tone Soloing for Bass Guitar

Voice Leading Jazz Guitar

Guitar Fretboard Fluency

The Circle of Fifths for Guitarists

First Chord Progressions for Guitar

The First 100 Jazz Chords for Guitar

100 Country Licks for Guitar

Pop & Rock Ukulele Strumming

Walking Bass for Jazz and Blues

Guitar Finger Gym

The Melodic Minor Cookbook

The Chicago Blues Guitar Method

Heavy Metal Rhythm Guitar

Heavy Metal Lead Guitar

Progressive Metal Guitar

Heavy Metal Guitar Bible

Exotic Pentatonic Soloing for Guitar

The Complete Jazz Guitar Soloing Compilation

The Jazz Guitar Chords Compilation

Fingerstyle Blues Guitar

The Complete DADGAD Guitar Method

Country Guitar for Beginners

Beginner Lead Guitar Method

The Country Fingerstyle Guitar Method

Beyond Rhythm Guitar

Rock Rhythm Guitar Playing

Fundamental Changes in Jazz Guitar

Neo-Classical Speed Strategies for Guitar

100 Classic Rock Licks for Guitar

The Beginner's Guitar Method Compilation

100 Classic Blues Licks for Guitar

The Country Guitar Method Compilation

Country Guitar Soloing Techniques